BIGGEST and SMALLEST!

GUINNESS WORLD RECORDS

D0051824

BIGGEST and SMALLEST!

GUINNESS WORLD RECORDS

by CHRISTY WEBSTER

HARPER
An Imprint of HarperCollinsPublishers

GUINNESS WORLD RECORDS: OFFICIALLY AMAZING

Since 1955, Guinness World Records has been the world's most trusted, accurate, and recognized source for record-breaking achievements. From the smallest dog to the largest arcade machine to the tallest ice-cream cone, Guinness World Records is home to big, small, short, tall, long, wide, and Officially Amazing record holders of all sizes.

Guinness World Records: Biggest and Smallest!
© 2016 Guinness World Records Limited.
The words GUINNESS WORLD RECORDS and related logos are
trademarks of Guinness World Records Limited.
Image of Heaviest Pumpkin (page 60) © epa/Alamy.

Library of Congress Control Number: 2015952905
ISBN 978-0-06-234178-5

Design by Victor Joseph Ochoa and Sean Boggs
15 16 17 18 19   PC/RRDC   10 9 8 7 6 5 4 3 2 1
❖
First Edition

SECTION ONE:

ASTOUNDING ANIMALS

Have you ever seen a horse as tall as a professional basketball player? How about a dog smaller than your shoe? Have you ever wondered just how long a cat's fur can grow? Turn the page to see the biggest beasts and the littlest critters in the world!

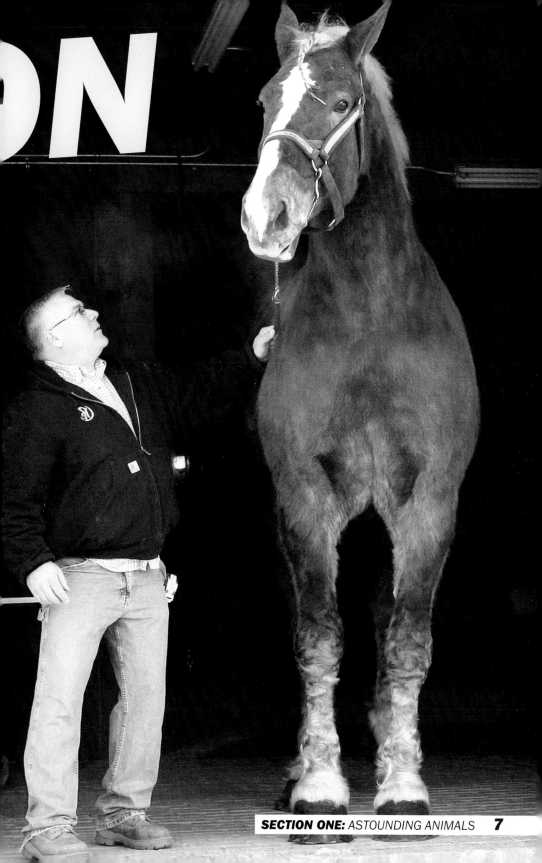

FROM TIP TO TAIL!

Mon Ami von der Oelmühl, an Irish wolfhound, was named the **longest dog** in the world in 2006, stretching over 7.5 feet from nose to tail.

The **longest dog ever** was Aicama Zorba of La-Susa from the UK. The Old English mastiff was 8 feet, 3 inches long, and he was also the **heaviest dog ever** at 343 pounds.

The most recent **longest dog** was Farrell, a male Irish wolfhound, who measured 7 feet, 9.17 inches from nose to tail tip. Owned by Robert and Kate Fandetti of Baneberry, Tennessee, he sadly passed away in February 2014. The search is currently ongoing to find his replacement.

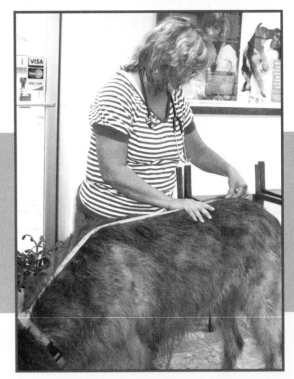

Heaven Sent Brandy is the **shortest dog** in length. She is only 6 inches from her nose to the tip of her tail. It would take 15 Heaven Sent Brandys to reach the length of Mon Ami (see opposite). But, of course, she is one of a kind!

FURRY FACTS

Lizzy, a Great Dane, is the **tallest female dog** in the world. She measures 3 feet, 1.9 inches tall at the shoulder and lives in Alva, Florida, with her owner, Greg Sample.

Zeus, the **tallest dog ever**, was even taller at 3 feet, 8 inches! The Great Dane from Michigan was named after the king of the gods in Greek mythology. Sadly, he passed away in September 2014.

The **shortest dog** in height is a Chihuahua named Miracle Milly, who lives in Puerto Rico. When she was born, she fit into a teaspoon. Now she stands at 3.8 inches tall. You would need 11 Millys standing in a tower to be as tall as Zeus, the tallest dog ever!

The Old English mastiff is the **heaviest dog breed** in the world. They can weigh up to 200 pounds, more than an average grown man!

Cupcake is the **smallest service dog** in the world! She lives in New Jersey and is only 6.25 inches tall. But she has a big impact. She visits sick and injured people in hospitals and nursing homes, bringing them hope and cheer.

The **smallest police dog** is Midge. She is a Chihuahua–rat terrier mix who works as a police dog in Ohio, even though she is only 11 inches tall.

Bebe is the **smallest dog model**. At only 6.7 inches tall, this long-haired Chihuahua knows how to strut her stuff.

HEAR! HEAR!
The **biggest ears on a living dog** belong to Harbor, a coonhound who lives in Colorado. Each ear is over a foot long—12.25 inches on the left and 13.5 inches on the right.

A bloodhound named Tigger had the **longest ears on a dog ever**. His left ear was 13.5 inches, but his right ear was even longer—13.75 inches! He used to trip over his ears as a pup.

Puggy is a Pekingese who lives in Texas, and he has the **longest tongue on a living dog**. His tongue measures 4.5 inches from his snout to the tip.

The **longest dog tongue ever** belonged to Brandy, a boxer who lived in Michigan. Her tongue was 17 inches long!

The **longest eyelash on a dog** belongs to Ranmaru, an Australian labradoodle from Japan. It was measured in September 2014 at 6.69 inches long.

MORE FURRY FACTS:

An Irish wolfhound named Finnegan holds the record for **longest tail on a dog**—28.46 inches!

The **largest wild dog** ever was Hayden's bone-crushing dog, which went extinct over five million years ago. It lived in North America for 15 million years. It looked a little like a hyena, and scientists estimate that it could have weighed up to 374 pounds.

The **largest wild cat** is still alive today. The Siberian Tiger can weigh up to 675 pounds.

The world's **heaviest ball of dog hair** weighed 201 pounds. It was gathered from 8,126 dogs by the Texas Hearing and Service Dogs.

Sophie Smith has the **longest fur on a cat**—10.11 inches. She surpassed the previous record holder's measurement by more than an inch! Rescued when she was just a kitten, Sophie lives in Oceanside, California.

ME-WOW!

The **tallest domestic cat ever** was Savannah Islands Trouble, or Trouble for short. He was 19 inches tall and lived in Nevada.

The **longest domestic cat ever** was Stewie, a Maine coon who lived in Nevada and stretched to over 4 feet long (48.5 inches, to be exact).

Stewie also held the record for **longest tail**. His tail alone was 16.34 inches long!

The record for **longest whiskers on a domestic cat** belongs to Missi, a Maine coon who lives in Finland. Her whiskers are 7.5 inches long.

The competition for **shortest cat** is pretty stiff. In 2010, Fizz Girl held the record at just 6 inches tall. But in 2013, a munchkin cat named Cye challenged her with his 5.35-inch stature.

The current record holder is Lilieput (pictured), a nine-year-old female munchkin cat, who measures 5.25 inches from the floor to the shoulders.

But all these little kitties would tower over the **shortest cat ever**. Tinker Toy was a Himalayan-Persian mix who stood only 2.75 inches tall!

Domestic cats have even bigger cousins, of course! The **largest living cat** is Hercules. He's a liger—a mix between a tiger and a lion. He stands 4 feet, 1 inch tall and weighs 922 pounds! He has a brother named Sinbad who is even taller—but Hercules still holds the record because he's heavier.

FACT!

Some big cats used to have big teeth. The cat who had the **largest fangs compared with its body size** was the Eusmilus which lived over 29 million years ago. Its body was about the size of a leopard, but its canine teeth were 6 inches long, almost as long as its whole skull.

Big Jake in Wisconsin is the **tallest living horse**. Without shoes, Big Jake is 82.75 inches tall—just shy of 7 feet, and that's just to his shoulder!

Thumbelina is the **shortest horse**. The miniature sorrel brown mare is just 17.5 inches high!

The **shortest male horse** is Charly, a miniature Aragon Arabian horse who stands 25 inches tall.

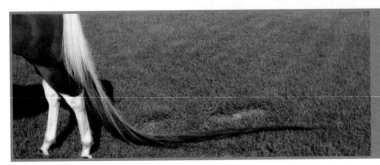

Summer Breeze in Kansas is the horse with the **longest tail**. Her tail trails behind her at 12 feet, 6 inches long.

Guess how little KneeHi got his name? He's the **shortest donkey**. The miniature Mediterranean donkey lives in Florida and is only a little over 2 feet tall at 25.29 inches.

FACT!

There's a breed of donkey whose hair grows at least 6 inches. The Baudet du Poitou donkey from France—also one of the largest breeds—holds the record for **donkey breed with the longest hair**. Its hair grows into a tangled, tattered coat over its lifetime.

At 5 feet, 8 inches tall, Romulus is the **tallest living donkey**. Romulus belongs to the well-named breed American Mammoth, and he lives in Texas with his brother Remus, who is only 2 inches shorter.

CARE TO TAKE THIS BULL BY THE HORNS?

The record for **largest horn circumference on a bull** was held by Lurch. The African Watusi bull belonged to Janice Wolf of Arkansas and had horns with a circumference of 3 feet, 1.4 inches. Sadly, Lurch passed in May 2010. A local taxidermist produced a life-size model to celebrate Lurch's impressive feat.

BARNSTORMING STATS:

Cute little Manikyam is the world's **shortest cow**, standing at just 24.07 inches from hoof to shoulder. Living in Kerala, India, with owner Akshay N.V., her record was verified on June 21, 2014.

The **shortest bull** is Chegs HHAR Golden Boy of California. In March 2014 he was measured at 28.2 inches from the hoof to the withers (the ridge between shoulder blades).

Cattle aren't the only ones with impressive horns. Uncle Sam from Pennsylvania had the **longest goat horns**. They were 52 inches (over 4 feet!) from the tip of one to the tip of the other.

GET YOUR GOAT RECORDS:

The world's **largest goat** was a British Sanaan named Mostyn Moorcock. He was 44 inches tall and 66 inches long.

The **largest litter of goats** was a litter of six born to a goat named Lucy in Pennsylvania in 2006.

And the **largest goat cheese** ever made weighed over 2,070 pounds, made by Ioannis Stathoris Ltd. of Greece in 2010.

The **largest sheep ever** was 43 inches tall—that's over 3.5 feet! He was a Suffolk ram from Oregon named Stratford Whisper 23H.

Horses, donkeys, cows, sheep, and goats—what other animals live on a farm? How about ants? The **largest ant farm** was almost 4 feet tall and almost 3 feet wide. It was actually a living advertisement! The gel ant farm lived inside a bus stop ad in the shape of a tooth. When the ants made tunnels in the gel, it looked like there were cavities in the tooth. What was it advertising? Anticavity toothpaste, of course.

FACT!
The **biggest ant** is the wingless queen of the fulvous driver ant, a species that lives in South Africa. The queen can grow to be almost 2 inches long.

The **largest millipede** is a full-grown African giant black millipede that lives in Texas. It's 15.2 inches long, 2.6 inches around, and—get this—it has 256 legs.

The **largest snail** in the world is the African giant snail. The largest recorded specimen, known as Gee Geronimo, was even longer than the longest millipede—15.5 inches. It weighed 2 pounds.

The **largest known spider** is the male Goliath bird-eating spider. Two separate specimens have been collected or raised that have had a leg span of 11 inches—so it could easily cover a dinner plate!

SENSATIONAL SPIDERS:

The **largest spiderweb ever built indoors** was discovered in an outhouse in the UK—it was 16 feet, 8 inches long and 12 feet, 6 inches wide. It was probably built by many common house spiders.

But that's nothing compared with the **biggest outdoor spiderweb**, covering an entire playing field at a school in the UK—it was over 11 acres in area.

The ogre-faced spider has the **largest spider eyes**—but they're still only one-twentieth of an inch across.

And the **largest spider egg**, laid by the genus *Mygalomorphus*, is the size of a small pea.

The bird that laid the **largest egg ever** was also the **largest bird ever**—the extinct Madagascar elephant bird. It laid eggs that were a full foot long and could hold over 2 gallons of liquid—as much as seven ostrich eggs or 183 chicken eggs. Or more than 12,000 hummingbird eggs.

FACT!
The **largest bird egg** is from an ostrich on a farm in Sweden. It laid an egg that weighed 5 pounds, 11 ounces.

The vervain hummingbird lays the **smallest egg of any bird**. The eggs are less than half an inch long and weigh about a hundredth of an ounce.

AVIAN ACHIEVEMENTS:

The **smallest bird** is the bee hummingbird of Cuba. The males are only 2.24 inches long, half of which is the beak and tail.

The **largest bird** is the North African ostrich, which can grow up to 9 feet tall.

Big Daddy, living at Sea Life Blackpool in the UK, is the crab with the **longest legs**. His longest leg is 4 feet, 8 inches long.

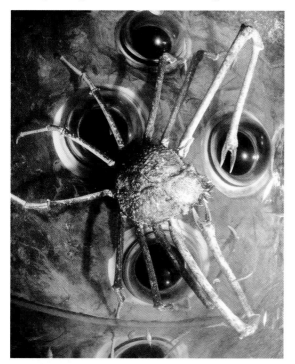

The **largest crocodile living in captivity** is Cassius, an Australian saltwater crocodile that lives in Marineland Melanesia in Australia. He's 17 feet, 11 inches long, weighs more than a ton, and is about 100 years old!

The **largest crocodile ever in captivity** was even bigger. Lolong was a saltwater crocodile that lived in the Philippines and was over 20 feet long.

The **biggest crocodile ever** was a prehistoric species called *Sarcosuchus imperator* from around 110 million years ago. According to fossils found in the Sahara Desert, this croc could grow to 37–40 feet!

Medusa just nabbed the record for the **longest snake ever in captivity**. She is a reticulated python that lives in Kansas City, Missouri. She is 25 feet, 2 inches long.

The **largest dinosaur museum** in the world is the massive Shandong Tianyu Museum of Nature in China. It's got over 300,000 square feet of exhibits and holds 1,106 dinosaur specimens and thousands of other fossils!

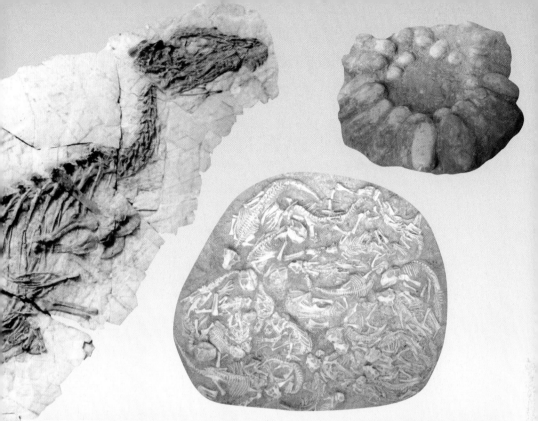

MORE DINO DETAILS:

The dinosaur with the **largest brain relative to its body** was the Troodontid. They were probably about as smart as the smartest birds.

The Hadrosaurid, or duckbill dinosaur, had the **largest dinosaur footprint—** examples found in Utah have been 4.5 feet long and 2.5 feet wide.

The **smallest dinosaur footprint** is almost smaller than you can believe. It's less than 1 inch from the heel to the tip of the longest toe. It was discovered in the UK and is from the Middle Jurassic period. The exact species is yet to be confirmed.

A set of 5,000-plus footprints in the Cal Orcko quarry in Bolivia stretches over 1,150 feet, making it the **longest dinosaur footprint trail**! The footprints were made by a therapod dinosaur around 68 million years ago.

The Shandong fossil bone bed in China set the record for the **biggest dinosaur fossil site**. It has already yielded more than 7,600 fossils from the late Cretaceous period.

ONE GIANT LEAP FOR DOGKIND

The world record for the **highest jump by a dog** is 5 feet, 7 inches. It was cleared by Cinderella May, a Holly Grey who lives in Florida.

Another high-jumping pup is Stag, who is the dog with the record for **highest jump by a dog, leap and scramble**. Stag—a lurcher from the UK—scaled a smooth wooden wall that was 12 feet, 2.5 inches high in 1993.

Dogs aren't the only pets that can jump. In 2013, Alley from Texas set the record for the **longest leap by a cat**—6 feet!

ON THE BALL!

The **fastest 10 meters traveled on a ball by a dog** was achieved by Purin from Japan. On January 31, 2015, the beagle covered 32 feet, 9 inches in 11.90 seconds. Multitalented Purin was really on a roll, because two months later she also claimed the record for **most balls caught with the paws in one minute**: 14!

Dogs don't just jump and roll—they can also surf! The **longest wave surfed by a dog in open water** was 351 feet, 8.4 inches. Abbie Girl set the record in California in 2011.

The **largest dog wedding ceremony** took place in Littleton, Colorado, in 2007. Tying the knot were 178 canine couples, who sealed their marriages with a bark.

SECTIO
TWO:

GREAT GAME CHANGERS

What's the biggest board game you can imagine? How small do you think the tiniest teddy bear in the world is? Turn the page to read about the biggest and smallest games and toys in the world!

AT THE CONTROLS!

You can't hold this in your hands. The **largest video game controller** is 12 feet long; 5 feet, 3 inches tall; and 1 foot, 8 inches deep! It works just like a normal Nintendo Entertainment Controller, even though it's 30 times bigger.

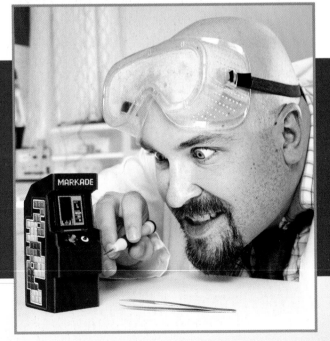

You could hold this arcade game in your hand—the entire thing will fit in your palm. The **smallest arcade machine** is 4.88 inches high, 2.05 inches wide, and 2.36 inches deep. You can play clones of Tetris, Space Invaders, and Breakout on it—as long as you are very careful!

The **largest arcade machine** is almost three times bigger than an average man. It stands 14 feet, 4.9 inches tall; 6 feet, 3.96 inches wide; and 3 feet, 5.6 inches deep. Created by Jason Camberis of Illinois, it features several classic games, including the ever-popular PAC-MAN.

If you like big video games, you'll like big board games, too! The **largest board game commercially available** is 6 feet, 5.6 inches long and 3 feet, 2.6 inches wide—about the size of a twin bed. It's called The War Game: World War II.

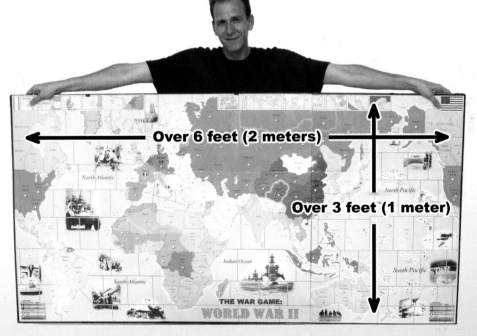

The **largest board game ever** would keep you entertained for hours—and that's before passing Go! In 2012, De Eindhovense School in the Netherlands created a Monopoly board that measured more than 2,421 square feet, complete with oversize hotels and houses. Not surprisingly, it also holds the record for **largest Monopoly board**.

Anyone for Twister? The **largest Twister board** was also in the Netherlands and spanned almost 24,000 square feet. It was created by participants at the University of Twente in Enschede, the Netherlands.

The **largest game of pick-up sticks** was achieved in Zimbabwe by four teams of 112 children. They played with 30 plastic sticks that were each almost 30 feet long!

YOU'RE GOING TO NEED A BIGGER BOARD

The **largest chess piece** is a king piece that measures 16 feet, 7 inches tall and 6 feet, 8 inches across at its base. It was created by Gitok School in Belgium and measured on April 4, 2014. It surpassed the previous record by a full 2 feet!

If you wanted to play a full game of giant chess, you'd have to go to Alberta, Canada. The **largest chess set** has a board that is 19 feet, 4 inches on each side, and the king piece is almost 4 feet tall.

FACT!
The **smallest commercially available 1,000-piece puzzle** is 7.17 by 10.12 inches. It's made by Standard Project Limited, the same Hong Kong company that makes the 500-piece smallest puzzle.

What's really tiny but has a lot of pieces? The smallest jigsaw puzzles! The **smallest commercially available jigsaw puzzle with 500–1,000 pieces** is only about the size of a sheet of notebook paper—it measures 8.27 by 11.65 inches. It's made in Hong Kong, has 500 pieces, and when completed it shows a picture of Peru's ancient mountain city of Machu Picchu.

How many pieces do you think were in the **jigsaw puzzle with the most pieces**? Ten thousand? Fifty thousand? Try 551,232 pieces! When it was completed, it was over 3,600 square feet in area. The students of the University of Ho Chi Minh City in Vietnam put it together. When finished, it showed a picture of a lotus flower, widely regarded as the country's national flower.

The **largest jigsaw puzzle** was even bigger. A lot bigger. When put together, it covered more than 58,435 square feet and took 777 people to assemble the 21,600 pieces at the former Kai Tak Airport in Hong Kong, China.

The **largest commercially available jigsaw puzzle in terms of area** is 9.05 by 6.29 feet and has 18,000 pieces.

The **largest commercially available jigsaw puzzle in terms of pieces** has 32,256! Both are made by the same company, Ravensburger AG in Germany.

Ever try to make a building out of playing cards? It's not easy. But pro card stacker Bryan Berg has proven that the sky's the limit. In 2010, he re-created a casino/hotel complex in Macau, China, with 218,792 cards, to achieve the **largest playing card structure**. Overall, it stretched more than 34 feet long and stood 9 feet, 5 inches tall. Just nobody sneeze, okay!

The **tallest house of cards** was also built by Bryan Berg! It was 25 feet, 9 inches tall, and he built it during the State Fair of Texas in 2007.

AMAZING MAZES

At more than 12,855 square feet in area, the **largest ice maze** was the Arctic Glacier Ice Maze, built in 2010 in Buffalo, New York. The walls were 6 feet tall and made of 2,171 ice blocks that each weighed 300 pounds.

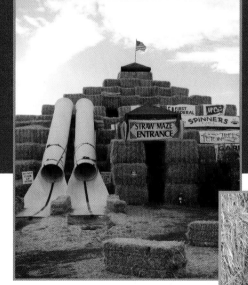

The **largest temporary straw-bale maze** was the Mega Maze in Idaho—it was an astonishing 96,847 square feet in area! It had tons of designs, including a 3D section and a pyramid. There were some sections—like a go-cart track and a kiddie maze—that weren't even included in the official measurements. The maze used 3,203 bales of straw and took three weeks to build.

The **largest permanent hedge maze** in the world is the Pineapple Garden Maze at the Dole Plantation in Hawaii. It has a total area of 3.15 acres. It also holds the record for the **longest path in a permanent hedge maze—** 13,001 feet!

Verified on October 3, 2014, the **largest temporary corn maze** covered 60 acres! It was grown by Cool Patch Pumpkins in Dixon, California.

TAKING TURNS, LOTS AND LOTS OF TURNS

The **longest path in a temporary corn maze** was created by Workgroup Labyrinth in Flanders, Belgium, in 2005. It included a path that wound its way across 10.45 miles!

The **largest piñata** ever was 47 feet high; 68 feet, 7 inches long; and 37 feet, 9 inches wide. It was built at the 69th Regiment Armory in New York, in the shape of a giant orange M&M candy standing on a cake to celebrate the first birthday of the release of the Pretzel M&M's.

The **largest number of piñatas displayed at the same time** was 504. They were on display in Mexico in 2008.

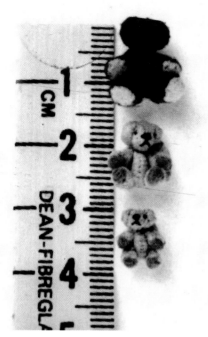

Too little to cuddle? No such thing. The **smallest commercially available stitched teddy bear** is 0.29 inches long. The microbears are made by Cheryl Moss in South Africa.

At the other end of the scale, the **largest stitched teddy bear** is more than 2,000 times larger. It's 55 feet, 4 inches long! It was displayed at the Exploration Place in Wichita, Kansas, and its name was C.T. Dreams, short for Connect the Dreams.

PUZZLED?
If you like colorful blocks, you'll also like this one. A Rubik's Cube is usually 3 by 3 by 3 squares, right? The **largest order of Rubik's Cube** is 17 by 17 by 17. The toy has 1,539 moving parts and was created for the New York Puzzle Party Symposium in 2011. Bet that would take a while to solve!

The **largest life-size house ever made from interlocking plastic bricks** is 15 feet, 4 inches high; 30 feet, 9 inches long; and 18 feet, 10 inches wide. It has two stories and four rooms. Twelve hundred volunteers built the house out of 2.4 million LEGO bricks in Dorking, United Kingdom.

This toy really rocks—the **largest rocking horse** is 40 feet, 3 inches long; 14 feet, 10 inches wide; and 26 feet, 10 inches tall. It was created by Gao Ming in Linyi, China.

The **largest Lite-Brite picture** was a mural of the phrase "Forever Saint Paul" in St. Paul, Minnesota. It was 9.5 feet tall and 23 feet long, and used 596,897 pegs.

The **longest usable golf club** measured 20 feet, 6 inches long. It was made by Michal Furrh of Dallas, Texas, who teed off to a new record on June 23, 2015, at the Rolling Hills Country Club in Arlington, Texas.

How many people can fit on one snowboard? Well, when it's the **largest snowboard** in the world, the answer is 27! The snowboard is 32 feet, 9.7 inches long and 7 feet wide, and took Arnold Schindler and his team in Switzerland 200 hours to build.

The **largest soccer ball** was displayed in Doha, Qatar, in 2013 and measures 125 feet, 8 inches all the way around! It weighs more than 2,116 pounds— try to kick that!

A GOOD PLACE TO GET YOUR KICKS

It might be more fun to try to kick the **largest collection of soccer balls**! Since 1995, Roberto Fuglini of Argentina has collected more than 861 different soccer balls.

It's always nice to get together with some people for a friendly game. And sometimes it's nice to get together with a lot of people for a gigantic game! The **largest game of Bingo** involved 70,080 players in Bogotá, Colombia, in 2006.

GAME ON . . . AND ON AND ON

The **largest game of Telephone** was in London, UK, in 2008. It took 2 hours and 4 minutes for 1,330 children to whisper a sentence to each other, one after the other. The sentence began as "Together we can make a world of difference" and morphed into "We're going to break a world record" before ending up as "Haaaaa!"

In 2011, 2,135 kids got together at Logan-Rogersville High School in Rogersville, Missouri, to play the **largest game of Duck, Duck, Goose**.

The **largest game of Simon Says** was made up of 12,215 people at the Utah Summer Games Opening Ceremony in 2007. This beats the previous record by 10,589! Simon—and Guinness World Records—says that's officially amazing.

This supersized toy will get you in a spin. . . . Over a period of three years, Beth Johnson, from La Rue, Ohio, built the **largest yo-yo**. It has a diameter of 11 feet, 9 inches and works just like a normal yo-yo . . . except it requires a crane to hang from rather than your hand!

SECTION THREE

FANTASTIC FOODS

From the state fair to the dinner table, there are some pretty big things to eat— and things to eat with! Turn the page to see some of the biggest foods and food creations in the world! And don't worry—your eyes are definitely bigger than your stomach when it comes to these record holders.

FOCUS ON: PETER GLAZEBROOK!

Peter Glazebrook isn't afraid to eat his vegetables. And good thing, too, because one of his skills as a gardener is growing some of the world's biggest vegetables. His backyard garden in Nottinghamshire, UK, has produced 10 Guinness World Records holders in the past 20 years, three of which are still current. In September 2014, Peter set the record for **heaviest carrot**. Measured at the Harrogate Autumn Flower Show, the vegetable weighed in at a staggering 20 pounds, 1.6 ounces.

In April 2014, Peter achieved the record for **heaviest cauliflower**. It weighed 60 pounds, 9.3 ounces.

And in September 2011, Peter claimed the record for **heaviest potato**. The spud was 8 pounds, 4 ounces, beating the previous record holder, at 7 pounds, 13 ounces.

The world's **longest carrot** is 19 feet, 1.96 inches long. It was grown by Joe Atherton of the UK in 2007.

The **heaviest avocado** was grown in Venezuela by Gabriel Ramirez Nahim and weighed 4 pounds, 0.83 ounces. That's almost ten times as much as an average avocado.

Scott Robb's **heaviest cabbage** weighed in at 138 pounds, 4 ounces at the Alaska State Fair in 2012.

The **longest cucumber** was 3 feet, 6.1 inches, and was also grown in Somerset, UK, by Ian Neale from Wales.

The **largest cucumber plant** grows in a special place—Walt Disney World's Epcot Science Project! It grows on a huge rectangular trellis, with the cucumbers hanging down. As of 2006, it covered an area of 610.31 square feet.

The **heaviest cucumber** weighed 27 pounds, 5.3 ounces. It was a zeppelin cucumber presented at the National Giant Vegetables Championship in Somerset, UK, in 2003. Alfie J. Cobb grew the cucumber and took second place in the competition!

The **largest tomato plant** covers an area of 919.88 square feet and was grown by Aleph Inc. at Tomato-no-mori in Ecorin-mura, in Japan. It was measured on November 10, 2013, the 350th day after the seed was planted. According to Aleph Inc., they had harvested 11,484 tomatoes from the plant up to the day of the measurement. This was the eighth year since they started cultivating tomato plants that are not grown in soil.

The **longest zucchini** is 7 feet, 10.3 inches. Gurdial Singh Kanwal of India grew it in his garden in Ontario, Canada.

The **heaviest zucchini** was 64 pounds, 8 ounces. It was grown by Bernard Lavery of Rhondda Cynon Taf in the UK. Dr. Lavery has held 26 world records throughout his gardening career and even wrote a book called *How to Grow Giant Vegetables*!

The **longest edible mushroom** measured 1 foot, 11.28 inches and was a *Pleurotus eryngli* grown by the HOKUTO Corporation. The fungus was measured at the company's Mushroom Research Laboratory in Nagasaki, Japan, on July 25, 2014, and it weighed in at more than 7 pounds, 14 ounces. Over the 66 days it took to grow the fantastic fungus, one of the greatest challenges faced was making sure the mushroom didn't fall and break under its own weight. Securing the record was the perfect way to celebrate the company's 50th anniversary!

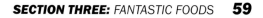

The **heaviest squash** weighed in at 1,486 pounds, 9.6 ounces. Grown by Canadian Joel Jarvis in 2011, the supersized vegetable was presented at the Port Elgin Pumpkinfest in Ontario, Canada.

Swiss farmer Ben Meier grew the **heaviest pumpkin**! It weighed 2,323 pounds, as verified by the Great Pumpkin Commonwealth on October 12, 2014.

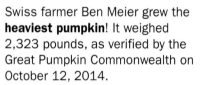

APPLES TO APPLES

The **heaviest apple** in the world was grown by Chisato Iwasaki in Hirosaki City, Japan, and weighed 4 pounds, 1 ounce. That's 13 times as heavy as the average apple.

Grown by Aharon Shemoel of Israel, the **heaviest lemon** tipped the scales at 11 pounds, 9.7 ounces in 2003. It never got lonely as its neighbor was also a supersized lemon!

The **largest orange** in the world measured 25 inches around at its widest point. It grew in Patrick and Joanne Fiedler's garden in Fresno, California, in 2006. Now that would make a lot of orange juice!

EGG-CELLENT EATS

Zakład Pakowania Jaj Mering of Poland cooked up 29,096 eggs to create the **largest serving of scrambled eggs**. The final portion weighed 3,452 pounds, 7 ounces. Overall the meal took 2 hours, 45 minutes to prepare.

The **largest omelet** in the world used 145,000 free-range eggs! Whipped up and fried by Ferreira do Zêzere City Council in Santarém, Portugal, in 2012, the final meal weighed in at a staggering 14,225 pounds, 6 ounces.

The world's **largest bagel** weighed in at 868 pounds. Made by Bruegger's Bagels in the USA, it was on display at the New York State Fair in August 2004.

Breakfast is the most important meal of the day, but you'd need a giant appetite to find your way to the bottom of this bowl. The world's **largest bowl of cereal** weighed 2,204 pounds, 10 ounces, and was served in a bowl that was 8 feet, 6 inches across and almost 5 feet tall. Kellogg's South Africa poured this serving of corn flakes in Johannesburg in July 2007.

The **largest cereal breakfast** in terms of attendance served an Australian cereal called Weet-Bix, Coco Pops, and Froot Loops. It took place in Tasmania, Australia, and involved 1,423 hungry cereal eaters.

A TREAT FOR ALL

If you prefer your cereal in "treat" form, this should be to your liking. On March 14, 2010, "MEGA BITES" Beyond Productions, Inc., in California made the **largest cereal treat**. It weighed 10,314 pounds and was made using 6,208 pounds, 1.28 ounces of marshmallow; 868 pounds, 8.96 ounces of butter; and 3,237 pounds, 5.76 ounces of Rice Krispies.

After a summer of barbecues and baseball games, you might have spent a lot of money on a lot of hot dogs. But Gorilla Tango Novelty Meats in Chicago can save you multiple trips! They sell the **largest hot dog commercially available**—for $40. This hot dog is 16 inches long, 4 inches in diameter, and weighs 7 pounds! Pass the ketchup, please!

The **longest hot dog** ever was made for Paraguay's 200th anniversary in 2011. The hot dog was 668 feet, 7.62 inches long, and sat in an equally lengthy bun. After the hot dog was measured, it was cut into pieces and eaten—by 2,000 people!

If that's still not enough hot dog for you, check out the **longest line of hot dogs**—it stretched 846 feet, 9.48 inches in Tokyo, Japan, in 2014.

In the barbecue of life, some people like the biggest hot dogs, but some prefer humongous hamburgers. The **largest hamburger commercially available** weighs 777 pounds. You can order it special from Juicy's Outlaw Grill in Corvallis, Oregon.

The **largest hamburger** ever made weighed 2,014 pounds and included hundreds of pounds of tomatoes, lettuce, onion, pickles, cheese, and bacon. It was prepared at Black Bear Casino Resort in Carlton, Minnesota, in 2012.

But maybe you're willing to sacrifice all those fixings and just go straight for the **largest hamburger patty** ever. That would yield you 6,040 pounds of beef. It was made at the Sleeping Buffalo Resort in Saco, Montana, in 1999. It took two hours to cook, and would have cost more than $7,000 if sold in a restaurant.

PIZZA PARTY

If you wanted to buy the **largest pizza**, you'd have to go to Big Mama's & Papa's Pizzeria in Los Angeles, California. For $199.99 plus tax, you can have a square pizza that is 4 feet, 6 inches on each side and can feed between 50 and 100 people. The pizza is called "The Giant Sicilian."

Some chefs pride themselves on spinning their pizza dough by hand. Tony Gemignani set the record for the **largest pizza base spun in 2 minutes**. The dough weighed 17.6 ounces and formed a pizza base measuring 33.2 inches when verified in April 2006.

Scott Wiener from New York City has the **largest collection of pizza boxes**. It contains 595 different boxes from 42 different countries.

Brian Dwyer of Philadelphia is also a pizza collector. He has the **largest collection of pizza-related items**, including games, puzzles, matchboxes, stickers, comic books, and clothing—in total, 561 items!

We've seen big round pizzas and big square pizzas, but how about a really long pizza? On June 20, 2015, the **longest pizza** measured more than 5,234 feet. It was created by three Italian companies—La Pizza+1 of Sante Ludovico, NIPfood of Dovilio Nardi, and Tomato World Week 2015—at Milan's Expo 2015 world fair. No special toppings were added—just 3,306 pounds of tomato sauce and 3,747 pounds of mozzarella!

SUPER SALAD

The **largest salad** ever made weighed 41,998 pounds. One thousand volunteers prepared the salad in Bucharest, Romania, in 2012, using tomatoes, cucumbers, lettuce, onions, bell peppers, carrots, olives, olive oil, and salt—delicious and nutritious!

The **largest fruit salad** was made by the Spar supermarket chain in Austria in 2014. It weighed 19,158 pounds, 2.72 ounces.

The **largest potato salad** weighed 7,224 pounds, 8 ounces and was made in Riga, Latvia.

Maybe a salad-and-soup combo would hit the spot? The **largest bowl of soup** was made in the Netherlands in 2009. It was 7,042.3 gallons and made from tomatoes, cucumbers, bell peppers, parsley, garlic, tomato paste, salt, pepper, olive oil, and basil.

The sandwich. The classic lunch food is also a world record holder. The **largest sandwich** to date weighed 5,440 pounds and contained corned beef, cheese, lettuce, mustard, and, of course, bread. It was made by Wild Woody's Chill & Grill in Roseville, Michigan in 2015.

The **largest bowl of pasta** ever weighed 13,786 pounds and was made by Buca di Beppo restaurant in Anaheim, California. It took five people 120 hours to make all that pasta and top it with 10 gallons of tomato sauce!

If you prefer baked pasta, there's the **largest lasagna** ever. Made in Poland in 2012, it weighed 10,725 pounds, 7 ounces. The lasagna was made in front of 5,000 people at the UEFA European Football Championship.

A special machine had to be used by the Gobierno Delegacional de Iztapalapa of Mexico to make the tortillas for the **largest enchilada**. It stretched 229 feet long and weighed more than 3,122 pounds. As per tradition, it was filled with chicken and salsa verde and topped with avocado, tomato, and onion.

The **largest serving of falafel** weighed 11,404 pounds, 8 ounces when verified in Beirut, Lebanon, in 2010. It took 300 student chefs to make it, and the dish it was served on broke the record for **largest ceramic plate**!

The **largest falafel** weighed 164.8 pounds. It was prepared by ten chefs at the Landmark Amman Hotel in Jordan, in 2012, and had a diameter of 51.1 inches.

The **largest cooked ham** was prepared in Italy in 2010. Two gigantic hams were cooked for 45 hours. The smaller ham weighed 175 pounds, but the bigger one took the record—182.87 pounds! The hams were cut up and shared as soon as they were unveiled. It took the hungry visitors only one hour to devour the first ham!

There's nothing fishy about this record . . . well, apart from the ingredients! Made by German chef Michael Gorich in 2009, **the largest fish stick** was 6 feet, 6 inches long and weighed more than 299 pounds!

Made in Castel di Lama in Italy, the **largest serving of meatballs** weighed 1,038 pounds, 6 ounces.

NOW THAT'S A MOUTHFUL!

The **largest single meatball** weighed 1,110 pounds, 7.84 ounces, measured 4 feet, 6.5 inches across, and was made in Columbus, Ohio. Seven people mixed the meat and spices in batches, packed it together, and baked it in an oven.

The **largest paella**—a traditional Spanish dish of rice, meat, seafood, vegetables, and spices—filled a pan that was 65 feet, 7 inches in diameter. Made by Juan Carlos Galbis and team in Spain, the 30-ton meal fed 100,000 people.

The record for **largest stir-fry** was achieved in 2011 in Amherst, Massachusetts. Chef Jet Tila made the 4,010-pound meal in a 14-foot frying pan.

The **largest box of popcorn** could hold 1,857 cubic feet. It took almost two hours to fill up in Osijek, Croatia, in 2011.

The **largest popcorn sculpture** was 11,688 pounds. It was made in Jamaica, New York, in 2006, by 50 people, and looked like a giant tiered cake.

If you like your popcorn in ball form, check out the **largest popcorn ball**. It weighed 3,423 pounds and was made by the employees of the Popcorn Factory in Lake Forest, Illinois, in 2006.

The **largest pretzel** weighed 842 pounds and was 26 feet, 10 inches long. It was made by Olaf Kluy and Manfred Keilwerth in Germany in 2008.

The **largest loaf of bread** weighed 3,463 pounds. It was baked by Joaquim Goncalves of Brazil in celebration of Guinness World Records Day in 2008.

The **largest slice of cheese** was created by Halayeb Katilo Co. in Egypt in 2012. It weighed 298 pounds, 11 ounces and measured 3 feet, 8 inches by 2 feet, 7 inches.

The **largest cheese sculpture** was made from 925 pounds of aged cheddar for the Wisconsin State Fair in 2011. The tasty, if unusual, artwork depicted a pig, a cow, a sprite, and a chicken all riding a roller coaster.

TIME FOR DESSERT!

The **largest cream-filled cookie** weighed 62 pounds, 4 ounces, and was 3 feet, 3 inches long by 2 feet, 3 inches wide. The cookie was made by Hoppe Food Group & Midden Brabant College in the Netherlands in 2011.

The **largest cookie** was 40,000 pounds of chocolate-chip goodness! It was made by the Immaculate Baking Company in North Carolina and covered an area of 8,120 square feet.

The **largest gingerbread man** weighed 1,435 pounds, 3 ounces. It was baked by IKEA Furuset in one piece in Oslo, Norway, in 2009.

Where would the largest gingerbread man live? In the **largest gingerbread house**! The edible home was baked and constructed in Bryan, Texas, by Traditions Club in 2013. It had a volume of more than 39,201 cubic feet and was built to raise money for a hospital.

Made by New Bremen Giant Pumpkin Growers in Ohio, the **largest pumpkin pie** was 20 feet wide and weighed 3,699 pounds. Ingredients included 1,212 pounds of canned pumpkin, more than 14 pounds of cinnamon, and 2,796 eggs!

The **largest wedding cake** was 15,032 pounds. It was made by chefs at the Mohegan Sun Hotel and Casino in Uncasville, Connecticut, in 2004.

Humans don't get to have all the dessert. The **largest cake for dogs** was more than 150 pounds. It had dog food inside and was shaped like a corgi, in celebration of the British royal wedding between Prince William and Kate Middleton in 2011.

WE ALL SCREAM FOR ICE CREAM!

The **tallest ice cream cone** measured 10 feet, 1.26 inches high. It was achieved by Hennig-Olsen Is AL and Trond L Wøien (both Norway) on July 26, 2015. After its record was confirmed, it was helicoptered from the factory to a racing event where it was dished out!

The **largest ice cream cake** weighed 22,333 pounds, 9.6 ounces. It was made from sponge cake, ice cream, frosting, and cookie crumbles by Dairy Queen in Toronto, Canada.

Some people like their ice cream in a boat, not a cone. The **largest ice cream boat** weighed 1,910 pounds, 4.8 ounces and was displayed in Stockholm, Sweden, in 2004.

If you'd rather have a pyramid-shaped dessert, there's a record for that too! Baskin-Robbins International created the **largest ice cream scoop pyramid** using 3,100 scoops of ice cream in Maui, Hawaii, in 2000. It weighed 800 pounds, stood 4 feet tall, and was comprised of 21 layers.

Did you know it was even possible to sculpt with this frozen dessert? The world's **largest ice cream sculpture** took the form of an 18th-century ship in Burbank, California, in 2002. It weighed more than 2,039 pounds and used 453.2 gallons of chocolate and vanilla ice cream. It was carved using a chain saw, hammer, and chisel. After it was unveiled, over 500 children ate it!

MORE TASTY ICE CREAM RECORDS:

The **most flavors of ice cream displayed together** is 985.
Ranging from vanilla to mango habañero, the display was created at
Crook's Palace Restaurant in Black Hawk, Colorado.

The **largest scoop of ice cream** weighed a mammoth 3,010 pounds. Ice cream
maker Kemps LLC used 733 tubs of strawberry ice cream to create the scoop.
It was displayed on June 28, 2014, as part of the Cedarburg Strawberry Festival.

The **largest ice cream sundae** weighed a whopping 54,917 pounds.
It was made at Palm Dairies Ltd. in Edmonton, Alberta, Canada.

The **largest iced coffee** was 1,500 gallons and used 3,000 pounds of ice. It was prepared by GourmetGiftBaskets.com in 2010.

The **largest cup of hot chocolate** was 880 gallons. It took 3 hours and 16 minutes to heat it up to a temperature of 104 degrees Fahrenheit at the Festival of Chocolate in Tampa, Florida, in 2013.

The **largest cup of coffee** was 3,758.7 gallons and was made by Caffé Bene in South Korea, in 2014.

Now we're in for a real treat—the biggest candies in the world! The record for **largest candy** is held by a butterscotch candy from Norway called a Smørbukk. It weighed 3,527 pounds, 6 ounces.

The scale of the **biggest jawbreaker** is truly jaw-dropping. It was 37.25 inches around, weighed 27 pounds, 12.8 ounces, and took 476 hours for Nick Calderaro of Canada to make.

The **biggest bubble-gum bubble** was 20 inches in diameter. Chad Fell from Alabama blew it in 2004 without using his hands.

BIG KISS

The **largest individual chocolate** was a Hershey's Kiss that weighed 30,540 pounds. It was displayed at Chocolate World in Hershey, Pennsylvania, in honor of the product's 100th anniversary in 2007.

The **largest box of chocolates** weighed 3,725 pounds and was made by Thorntons and Russell Beck Studios in London, UK, in 2008.

The **largest chocolate coin** weighed 1,450 pounds, 10 ounces and looked like a one-euro coin. It was made and displayed in Bologna, Italy, to celebrate Guinness World Records Day in 2012. Bet it was really rich!

The **largest chocolate bar by weight** tipped the scales at 12,770 pounds, 4.48 ounces and was made by British confectioner Thorntons.

The **largest chocolate bar by area**, meanwhile, was prepared by Marinko Biškić and Nadalina of Croatia (pictured). It covered 1,102.54 square feet when verified on April 11, 2015.

The **largest chocolate truffle**, weighing 1,768 pounds, 11 ounces, was made by Mirco Della Vecchia, Andrea Andrighette, Rimini Fiera, Fabbri 1905, Icam, and Martello in Rimini, Italy.

Sometimes chocolate is not just eaten—it's made into a gigantic work of art. The **largest chocolate candy sculpture** weighed 589 pounds, 8 ounces and was over 5 feet long. It was made for Valentine's Day in 2012 by Namba Walk of Japan.

The **largest chocolate sculpture** weighed 18,239 pounds, 8 ounces and was 6 feet tall. It looked like the Kukulkan pyramid in Chichén Itzá, Mexico, but was made in Irvine, California.

The **tallest chocolate fountain** stands 26 feet, 3 inches tall at the Bellagio Hotel and Casino in Las Vegas, Nevada. Two tons of chocolate flow through it at a rate of 120 quarts per minute.

All this giant food calls for giant utensils. The **largest chopsticks** in the world are 27 feet, 6 inches long. They are made from laquered pine tree trunks in Fukui, Japan, and took five months to complete.

Would you like ketchup on your giant food? Then you're going to need a pretty big packet! The **largest condiment sachet** measured 4 feet by 8 feet in Collinsville, Illinois. It was filled with 127 gallons of Heinz Ketchup.

The best place to eat all the largest foods is definitely the **largest restaurant** in the world. The Bawabet Dimashq Restaurant in Damascus, Syria, seats 6,014 diners and employs up to 1,800 staff.

It would have been pleasant to spend the afternoon at the **largest tea party**, which took place in Indore, India, in 2008. There were 32,681 people drinking tea at the same time!

A BIG BLOWOUT!

The **largest baking soda and vinegar volcano** stood 23 feet, 5 inches high when measured in Glencairn, Canada, on July 19, 2012. It was made from gravel and sand and filled with vinegar and food coloring. Then a backhoe scooped in the baking soda. The highest eruption reached 3 feet, 1 inch from the top of the volcano. Talk about blowing up big!

A papadum is a thin, crispy, round snack that is sometimes served with Indian food. The **tallest stack of papadums** stood 5 feet, 7 inches and was created by Tipu Rahman at the Tamarind Restaurant in Northampton, UK, on October 11, 2012. The stack contained 1,180 papadums.

The **tallest stack of pancakes** was made of 242 pancakes and measured a staggering 2 feet, 11 inches on October 16, 2014. It was achieved by the pancake restaurant within Efteling theme park in the Netherlands and bettered the previous record by a pancake-thin 0.6 inches!

Another fun thing to do with food is make decorations, like carving a pumpkin into a jack-o'-lantern. The **longest tunnel of jack-o'-lanterns** was created in Croton-on-Hudson, New York, in 2013, for the Great Jack-O'-Lantern Blaze. Called the Tunnel O' Pumpkin Love, it was made from 648 individually carved jack-o'-lanterns and was 20 feet long.

The **largest display of different fruit varieties** must have been a sight to see at the Zug Harvest Fair held in Switzerland in 2011. On show were 1,740 different kinds of fruit—mainly apples and pears.

PAINT THE TOWN RED

If you didn't want to just display food . . . you could throw it. The **largest food fight** is always on the last Wednesday in August in the town of Buñol, Spain. It's Tomatina, the annual tomato festival. In 2004, 38,000 people spent an hour throwing about 275,500 pounds of tomatoes at one another. By the end, the whole town is red with squished tomatoes.

Akiko Obata from Japan had the **largest collection of food related items**, which consisted of 8,083 fake food items, as of January 24, 2014. However tasty these treats may look, don't try to eat them. . . . They're all made of plastic!

A FEAST FOR THE EYES!

The **biggest bubble-gum mosaic** took five days to complete. It was a picture of Nelson Mandela and used about 100,000 pieces of bubble gum. Created in Johannesburg, South Africa, in the end it covered an area of 209 square feet.

The **largest cookie mosaic** was made from 16,390 MoonPie snack cakes and covered more than 1,358 square feet in area. It was made by 300 students of the Bright School in Chattanooga, Tennessee, in 2012.

The **largest doughnut mosaic** was created from 7,040 of the fried cakes in Lviv, Ukraine. Once the record had been verified, the doughnuts were handed out to the crowd.

The **largest nut mosaic**, created by the Lo Fung Art Gallery in Hong Kong in 2011, was more than 475 square feet in area, and used over 200,000 pistachio shells.

SECTION FOUR:

AMAZING ARTISTRY

From a 14-foot violin with a 17-foot bow to a pavement drawing that stretches for miles on end, these artists and performers have taken their creativity to the max. Turn the page to read about the biggest records in art and music.

STREET ART!

The **largest bottle-cap mosaic** was 33,626 square feet in area. It was built by the students at the Freiherr vom Stein School in Germany using 3,614,468 bottle caps.

The **largest ceramic mosaic** was named the *Hanoi Ceramic Mosaic Mural Project*, which coincided with the 1,000-year celebration of the establishment of Hanoi in Vietnam. It covers more than 16,901 square feet along the city stretches of the Red River Dike. Thirty-five artists from Vietnam and 10 other countries contributed to the mural.

Depicting the flag of the United Arab Emirates (UAE), pencils were used in a rather unusual way to make this giant artwork. Covering an area of 8,072.9 square feet, the **largest pencil mosaic** was created by Civil Defense General Command at Emirates Palace, in Abu Dhabi, UAE, on December 9, 2014.

The **largest seashell mosaic** is in Dubai, UAE, and is 1,873 square feet in area. It took 130 people 45 days to make the picture.

The students of Tsugeno High School in Japan used 1,620,840 toothpicks in seven different colors to make the **largest toothpick mosaic**. It covered more than 436 square feet.

That's not the only giant piece of art made of toothpicks. The **tallest toothpick sculpture** is 16.7 feet tall, and was achieved by Stan Munro at the Phelps Art Center in New York in 2013. Stan created a model of the Burj Khalifa, in Dubai, UAE, which is the world's **tallest building**.

The **largest toothpick sculpture** was of an alligator named Alley. It contained over 3 million toothpicks and stretched 15 feet long. The model croc was built by Michael Smith and measured in Louisiana in 2005.

You can also make giant sculptures out of matchsticks. The **largest matchstick structure** was called *Cathedrals of the Sea*. It was a model of a floating oil rig. It took over 15 years for David Reynolds of the UK to complete the sculpture, using some 4,075,000 matchsticks.

The **largest modeling balloon sculpture by a team** took the form of a supersized green darner dragonfly with a wingspan of 88 feet, 5 inches wide and body length of just over 70 feet. Using more than 6,800 balloons, the megabug was built over five days by balloon artist Brian Getz and his team at the Indiana State Museum in Indianapolis on June 12, 2015.

FACT!
The **largest balloon drop** happened at the Titanic Centenary Commemorations in Adelaide, Australia. 109,183 balloons were dropped.

As their name would suggest, LEGO® Minifigures are generally on the small side, standing just over an inch high. But at the Brick exhibition held in London, UK, in November 2014, you could have seen a monster Minifigure 150 times the size of the standard toy. Standing a colossal 19 feet, 18 inches tall, the sculpture was made from 1,985 balloons by Larry Moss and his team, easily claiming the record for **largest LEGO Minifigure made from modeling balloons**.

Created by the Salem Lutheran School in Orange, California, the **largest papier-mâché sculpture** was an amazing 28 feet, 1 inch around and was a model of Earth.

The planet Earth plus the whole solar system was the subject of the **largest 3D button sculpture**. It was displayed at the People's Museum in Newcastle-upon-Tyne, UK. The model was made out of 1,163,342 buttons.

2000

TWENTIETH CENTURY

1900-2000

VICTORIAN

1800-1900

10th CENTURY-
GEORGIAN
1000-1800

ENVIRONMENTALLY FRIENDLY ART!

You can create a sculpture out of almost anything. The **largest sculpture made from plastic bottles** was built by Jolanta Smidtiene of Lithuania. It was displayed in the Town Hall Square in the country's capital city, Kaunas, in 2011. It was a 52-foot Christmas tree made from 42,000 green bottles!

This life-size ship is the **largest polystyrene sculpture**—the stuff that white foam coffee cups are made of! It was 60 feet, 4 inches long; 14 feet, 9 inches wide; and more than 42 feet tall. It took 15 people at the Red Sea Mall in Saudi Arabia 36 hours to construct.

If you like to clean, you'll like this: the **largest soap sculpture**. It looks like a globe held by two hands, contains around 429 cubic feet of soap, and was built in Johannesburg, South Africa.

The **largest sculpture made of magnets** is very attractive. It's a 2-foot-5-inch-tall model of a Golden Globe Award, made by Nano Magnetics of Canada in 2011.

Most paintings are typically made on dry land, but the **largest painting completed underwater** was created by Danish artist Jesper Kikkenborg. He worked in a tank at the National Aquarium of Denmark on October 19, 2014. The picture depicted a marine woman with octopus tentacles for hair!

Most paintings are typically made with the hands, but not this one! The **longest line of footprints** consisted of 15,200 painted prints. The path wound 14,711 feet through Perth, Australia, as part of an event organized by WA Newspapers.

CHALK IT UP!

The **largest chalk pavement art** (pictured) measured 200,187.2 square feet. It was achieved by Danish art association Soulwash in Copenhagen, Denmark, on August 16, 2015. An estimated 25,000 people contributed to the chalk masterpiece, which featured everything from flowers to Minions!

The **largest display of chalk pavement art** consisted of 308 drawings at an event organized by Uozu Young Entrepreneurs Group of Japan on October 12, 2014.

The **longest chalk pavement art** stretched for 18,372 feet, 8 inches along Stadtrodaer Street in Jena, Germany. The street was closed so that 5,000 students could fill the pavement with their drawings.

An anamorphic painting is a two-dimensional image that looks as though it could be in 3D. The **largest anamorphic pavement art** (pictured) covered an area of 28,330.5 square feet. Qingdao International Horticultural Exposition 2014, Qingdao Shiyuan (Group) Co. Ltd., and the Art Academy of Qingdao Technological University of China completed the piece in just over two months on December 23, 2014.

The **largest anamorphic painting**, titled *The Rhythm of Youth*, measured 28,232 feet, 50.4 inches squared. It was created by Yongchun Yang and Yanting Xu (both from China) and was unveiled at Communication University of China, Nanjing, on June 11, 2014.

The residents of Bethel, Maine, built the **tallest snowman** (well, technically a snow-woman) in the world over the course of a whole month. It was 122 feet 1 inch tall, and nicknamed Olympia!

The world's **smallest snowman** is only 10 micrometers across. It was created by scientists at the National Physical Laboratory in the UK. Scientists used a tiny ion beam to draw the snowman's face.

The **largest paper crane** has a wingspan of 268 feet, 9 inches. It took 800 people to build the huge origami beast in Hiroshima, Japan.

The world's **largest Rube Goldberg machine**—a contraption designed to use a lot of steps to achieve one task— takes 300 steps to blow up and then pop a balloon in under two minutes.

The **largest drum kit** is over five times the size of a regular drum set. The bass drum alone on this set is 9 feet, 6 inches tall. The entire kit was built by Austrian percussion band Drumartic in 2012 and can be used to make music.

The **drum set with the largest number of drums** has 813 different pieces and belongs to Mark Temperato of Lakeville, New York. It takes a team of four people over 20 hours to set it up!

ONE-AND-A-TWO!

The **largest drum lesson** ever involved 1,651 participants. That must have been pretty loud! World Arts Multi-culture Inc. drummed up the record in Brisbane, Australia, in 2012.

The **largest saxophone** in the world that can be played by a single person is 22 feet, 1.55 inches long. The opening of the bell is 1 foot, 3.39 inches across. It was built by artisan company J'Elle Stainer of Brazil.

The **largest violin** is 14 feet long, and the bow used to play it is even longer at 17 feet. It was made by 15 master craftsmen from Markneukirchen, Germany.

FACT!
A total of 4,645 children from Chinese Taipei added another string to their bow in 2011, claiming the record for **largest violin ensemble**.

Created by Venter-Glocken of Germany, the **largest cowbell ensemble** involved 640 people. They played together in Switzerland in 2009.

The **largest steel cowbell** is 10 feet, 9 inches tall and weighs 2,028 pounds. Wouldn't you like to see the cow that can wear this one?

Benny J. Mamoto built the **largest trumpet** in 2009. It is 104 feet, 11.84 inches long. The bell alone is 17 feet across!

The **largest trumpet ensemble** involved 1,166 players at a concert in Bolivia in 2006. It was part of a larger concert that involved around 5,000 different instruments.

Have you ever seen a vuvuzela, the noisy plastic trumpets that are sometimes sold at sporting events? The **largest vuvuzela** is 114 feet, 9 inches long. The huge instrument was sounded at the beginning of each match during the 2010 FIFA World Cup in South Africa.

The **most people blowing vuvuzelas at the same time** was 12,511. This was also at a soccer match, in Port Elizabeth, South Africa, in 2009.

As well as the **largest trumpet**, Benny J. Mamoto can also boast the record for building the **largest xylophone**. It was 26 feet, 3 inches long and 8 feet, 2.4 inches tall.

The **largest xylophone ensemble** was 1,223 players. They played together at the North Sulawesi Art and Culture Festival in Tondano, Indonesia, in 2009, along with the **largest xylophone** (left)!

The **largest playable accordion** is 8 feet, 3.5 inches tall; 6 feet, 2.75 inches wide; 2 feet, 9.5 inches deep; and weighs approximately 440 pounds. The instrument, built by Giancarlo Francenella of Italy, bears the name Fisarmonica Gigante and was completed in 2001.

A collaboration between the China Accordion Association and the Shenzhen Accordion Association on July 20, 2014, achieved the **largest accordion ensemble**. A total of 1,361 accordion players performed with their instruments for just over five minutes to set the record.

The **largest electric guitar** in the world is 43 feet, 7.5 inches tall; 16 feet, 5.5 inches wide; and weighs 2,000 pounds. Modeled on a 1967 Gibson Flying V and built to a scale of 1:12, it was made by students from Conroe Independent School District Academy of Science and Technology in Texas, at a cost of $3,000. With construction beginning in October 1999, the instrument was finally played at the Cynthia Woods Mitchell Pavilion on June 6, 2000 with the opening chord of "A Hard Day's Night" by the Beatles.

SECTION FIVE:

VAST VEHICLES

Great hulking trucks, miniature motorcycles, and the big, big things that some vehicles can do will keep your imagination running! Turn the page to read all about these mighty machines.

WHEELY BIG!

The **largest monster truck** has held its record for quite some time. Bigfoot 5 is 15 feet, 6 inches tall with 10-foot tires. It weighs 38,000 pounds and was built in the summer of 1986 by Bob Chandler. It's now permanently parked in St. Louis, Missouri.

Big monster trucks can achieve big feats, too. The **longest ramp jump by a monster truck** is 214 feet, 8 inches, jumped by driver Dan Runte in Bigfoot 18.

Built by Russ Mann, the **longest monster truck** is 32 feet long and has held its record only since October 2014.

The **tallest limousine car** stands at 10 feet, 11 inches. It sits on eight monster-truck tires and has two separate engines. It was built by Gary and Shirley Duval of Australia.

A 100-foot-long, 26-wheeled limousine was designed by Jay Ohrberg of Burbank, California, making it the **longest car**. It has many features, including a swimming pool with a diving board and a king-size water bed.

The **heaviest limousine** is called Midnight Rider, designed by Michael Machado and Pamela Bartholomew. It weighs a whopping 50,560 pounds. It can hold up to 40 passengers and is built to look like a train car on the inside.

The **tallest rideable motorcycle** measures 16 feet, 8.78 inches from the ground to the top of the handlebars. It's six times as big as a normal motorcycle and took only six months for Italian engineer Fabio Reggiani to build.

The **heaviest rideable motorcycle**, known as the Panzerbike, weighs 10,470 pounds and was made by Tilo and Wilfried Niebel of Germany.

At the other end of the scale, the **smallest motorcycle** has a rear wheel that's only 0.86 inches across and a front wheel that's even smaller. Nevertheless, its builder, Tom Wiberg of Sweden, rode it 32 feet, 9.6 inches in order to qualify for the record. The seat height is only 2.55 inches and the fastest it can go is 1.24 miles per hour.

These aren't the kinds of tricycles you rode as a kid! They're like giant motorcycles with three wheels. The **heaviest rideable trike** was made in the Netherlands by Wouter van den Bosch and weighs over 1,650 pounds.

The **longest trike** is 26 feet, 7 inches long. It was built to serve as a mobile grandstand for a Swiss carnival band named Guggä-Rugger Buus.

The **largest mining truck body** is the Belaz 75710 manufactured by Belaz of Belarus. It has a volume of 22,792 cubic feet and can hold a total weight of 992,880 pounds. It also holds the record for **highest payload capacity**.

The **largest land vehicle** is the MAN TAKRAF RB293 bucket wheel excavator from Germany that weighs 31.3 million pounds. It has 18 buckets attached to a giant wheel, which helps it dump over 8 million cubic feet of earth onto a conveyor belt every day.

The **smallest roadworthy car** is only 25 inches high and a little over 2 feet wide. Painted to look like a military aircraft from World War II, it can drive on public roads that have a speed limit of up to 40 miles per hour.

The **largest loop-the-loop in a car** was achieved by Mattel. Hot Wheels created a life-size replica of their toy loop that was 60 feet in diameter, using 125 tons of plywood and steel. Drivers drove sealed-up cars through the loop in Los Angeles.

The **largest loop-the-loop by a remote-controlled model vehicle** is 10 feet, 5 inches in diameter. It was achieved by *The Gadget Show* in the UK, using a toy dirt bike.

The **tallest tire stack** is 19 feet, 11.4 inches and was achieved by Tire Discounters Inc. in Cincinnati, Ohio, in 2014. They used 25 tires to build the stack.

You can even make big artwork out of cars—the **largest car mosaic** was created with 460 Volkswagen cars!

The **smallest aircraft that could carry a passenger** was a biplane, *Bumble Bee Two*. It was only 8 feet, 10 inches long and had a wingspan of 5 feet, 6 inches. In 1988, *Bumble Bee Two* crashed and was destroyed. Fortunately, the plane's builder and pilot, Robert Starr, fully recovered from his injuries.

The **largest aircraft by wingspan** was the Hughes H4 Hercules flying boat, also known as the *Spruce Goose*. It had a wingspan of 319 feet, 11 inches. Millionaire Howard Hughes himself flew it 70 feet into the air in a test run in 1947, but it never flew again.

The **smallest jet aircraft** is a Bede BD-5J Microjet in San Juan, Puerto Rico. It weighs only 358 pounds and has a wingspan of 17 feet, but it can still reach speeds of 300 miles per hour.

HIGH FLIERS!

This is one way to miss the rush-hour traffic! Made by the Gen Corporation of Japan, the GEN H-4 is the **smallest helicopter**. It weighs 154 pounds, 5.1 ounces and has a top speed of 59 miles per hour. It can carry just one passenger and has a rotor length of just 13 feet.

FACT!

The **largest biplanes** were four aircraft built in 1918. They each had a wingspan of 126 feet and weighed 26,400 pounds.

The **largest paper aircraft**, with a wingspan of 59 feet, 8.93 inches, was built by fourteen students and employees of the Braunschweig Institute of Technology in Germany. It took the builders 1,200 hours to construct it.

Built by Markus Frey of Switzerland the **largest wingspan on a model aircraft** is 49 feet, 2 inches. It can fly up to a height of 500 feet!

Sometimes tiny vehicles can overcome their small scale by working in numbers. The **heaviest train car hauled by model locomotives** weighed 103,617 pounds and was pulled by 200 electric model engines.

A lot of these big and little vehicles have electric motors. None of them have a motor as small as the **smallest electric motor**, though. It's only 0.000000039 inch (1 nanometer) across. You need a microscope to use it—or even see it—at Tufts University in Massachusetts!

HOLD ON TO YOUR HATS!

Bet you would like to speed down a hill on this with your pals! The **largest snow sled** is 32 feet, 9 inches long; 13 feet, 1 inch wide; and 10 feet, 2 inches tall. It is now on permanent display in the town of Bergün, Switzerland, where it was made.

The **tallest rideable bicycle** is called Stoopidtaller and measures 20 feet, 2.5 inches from the ground to its handlebars. To qualify for the record, it had to be ridden at least 328 feet, 1 inch. Luckily the bike's builder and rider, Richie Trimble from the US, didn't fall off!

It'd be even harder to balance on the **tallest rideable unicycle**—that one is 10 feet, 1.26 inches. The owner of the unicycle, Mushegh Khachatryan of Armenia, rode it over 82 feet.

You've probably heard of a stretch limo, but how about a stretch bike? The **longest true bicycle**— with only two wheels and no stabilizers—is 117 feet, 5 inches long. It was built by members of the Mijl Van Maers Werkploeg in the Netherlands in 2011.

The **largest skateboard** is 36 feet, 7 inches long and 8 feet, 8 inches wide. It sits on wheels that are almost 9 feet across and was built by Rob Dyrdek and Joe Ciaglia in Los Angeles!

The **tallest useable pogo stick** is 9 feet, 6.5 inches tall. To qualify for the record, the jumper, Fred Grzybowski, had to bounce on the giant pogo stick at least 20 times in a row!

Grzybowski used to hold the record for **shortest pogo stick**, too—but he was overtaken by Ashrita Furman, who rode on a pogo stick only 18.16 inches high in February 2014!

The **largest skateboard lesson** was held in California in June 2012. It involved 311 participants!

The **smallest submarine** was comically called *BIG* and had a displacement of 1,366 pounds, 14.4 ounces. It was made by Pierre Poulin of Canada and could hold only one person. To qualify for the world record, the sub stayed submerged for 43 minutes.

The **largest sub** was 42,000 times as big as the smallest! The Russian 941 Akula had a displacement of over 58 million pounds!

And the **heaviest ship pulled by teeth** weighed 1,269,861 pounds. Omar Hanapiev of Russia pulled the *Gunib* for 49 feet, 2.4 inches using a rope connected only to his gnashers.

FACT!
The **largest ship ever**, the *Mont*, weighed 622,545 tons.

The **heaviest vehicle pulled on land over 100 feet** weighed 126,200 pounds. Rev. Kevin Fast hauled the giant fire truck on live television to set the record.

Maybe you can believe someone could pull a vehicle—but how about balancing one on your head? John Evans of the UK held a gutted Mini Cooper, weighing 352 pounds, on his head, setting the record for **heaviest car balanced on the head**.

SECTION SIX:

COOL CURIOSITIES

Why do people build the biggest and smallest things? Sometimes there isn't a practical reason—sometimes it's just for fun, to have something cool to look at, or a great big place to visit. Turn the page to see some of the most unusual biggest and smallest curiosities from around the world.

FACT!

Here it is, the classic world's-biggest record—the **largest ball of string**. It measures 41 feet, 6 inches around.

The **biggest ball of plastic wrap** weighs 470 pounds and is 10 feet, 7 inches around.

The **biggest ball of magnetic tape** weighs 1,256 pounds and is 6 feet, 7 inches tall. Students from all over the UK gathered to make the ball over a period of three weeks. If the tape was completely stretched out, it would reach from London to New York!

The **longest rubber band chain** by an individual measures 1.32 miles long and was made by Allison Coach. Each band was just 3.5 inches long.

MEET MEGATON

Here's another classic. . . . The **largest rubber-band ball** bounced into the record books with a weight of 9,032 pounds. Made by Joel Waul, the creation contains around 700,000 bands and was nicknamed Megaton.

This is rich—the **largest coin** weighs more than 2,231 pounds and measures 2 feet, 7.49 inches across. It's made of 99.99% pure gold and has a face value of AUS $1 million. They call it the 1 Tonne Australian Kangaroo because it features a picture of the country's famous marsupial.

The **largest temporary coin mural** used 2,546,270 one-yen coins (worth around $25,000 in total) and was more than 12,896 square feet in area. The mural in Saitama, Japan, was a portrait of John Lennon to promote love and peace.

The **largest permanent coin mural** uses 110,000 10-won coins (about $1,080) to display the flag of South Korea. It is 258 square feet in area.

The **smallest paper money** was the 10-bani note in Romania in 1917. It was only a little over 1.5 square inches in area—about one-tenth the size of a current $1 bill.

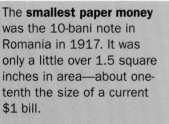

FACT!
The **largest paper money ever issued** was the one-kuan note during the Chinese Ming Dynasty more than 600 years ago. They were 117 square inches in area!

How many coins do you think you could collect? The **largest accidental hoard of coins** probably had around 60 million coins! It was accidental because the Spanish Plate Fleet sank off the coast of Florida in 1715, bringing the coins with it.

The **largest lottery prize fund** is Spain's Christmas lottery, nicknamed "El Gordo," which means "the Fat One." The 2012 jackpot was 2.52 billion euros, or about $3.32 billion.

The **largest piggy bank** was 26 feet, 4.3 inches long and 18 feet, 3.7 inches tall and was achieved by German Bank Kreissparkasse Ludwigsburg on May 18, 2015. A small crane had to be used to drop coins into it.

The world's **biggest ruby**, which weighs more than 48 pounds. Due to its unprecedented size, it has been nicknamed the King Ruby.

The **largest bar of gold** weighs 551 pounds, 2 ounces and was made by Mitsubishi Materials Corporation of Japan in 2005.

The **largest collection of telephones** contained 1,135 phones as of August 2011. Owner Michael Phillips of the US has them on display in his house in Greenville, South Carolina.

The **largest operational telephone** was 8 feet, 1 inch tall and 19 feet, 11 inches long, and weighed more than 7,716 pounds. The 23-foot, 5-inch receiver had to be lifted with a crane in order to make a call. It was displayed in 1988 in the Netherlands.

In contrast, the **smallest operational telephone** was only 1.8 inches long on its longest side and was made by Jan Piotr Krutewicz from the US.

If you wanted to go on a *big* camping trip, you would need the **largest sleeping bag**. The 54-foot-long, 175-pound sleeping bag is about 10 times the size of a regular sleeping bag.

If you wanted to roast marshmallows, you'd need the **largest matchstick** to light your campfire! It was 20 feet, 5 inches in length and was carved by Estonian Match Ltd. Nobody has yet to match this feat since 2004!

KNOW ANY GOOD CAMPFIRE SONGS?

The **largest bonfire** had a volume of 151,288 cubic feet when it was lit in Duindorp, Netherlands, on December 31, 2014.

The **biggest flashlight** is 13 feet, 1 inch long, and its light is comparable to 250 light bulbs. Built by Zweibrüder Optoelectronics of Germany, it took 230 hours to create.

The **largest glow stick** to date was 9 feet, 10 inches tall and glowed for about 10 minutes. It was created by glow stick manufacturer KNIXS of Germany.

You could say these record-breakers saw the light in 2011. The **largest glow stick design** was achieved by 2,972 students and depicted the well-known Cathedral of Learning building in Pittsburgh, Pennsylvania. They maintained the illuminated picture for four minutes.

The snakelike **longest chain of glow sticks** consisted of 9,021 glow sticks and stretched for 6,301 feet, 2.02 inches. It was created by students of the Attadale Primary School and their parents in Western Australia on October 25, 2014.

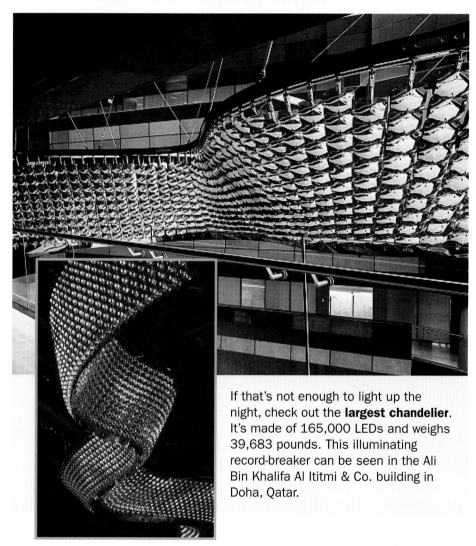

If that's not enough to light up the night, check out the **largest chandelier**. It's made of 165,000 LEDs and weighs 39,683 pounds. This illuminating record-breaker can be seen in the Ali Bin Khalifa Al Ititmi & Co. building in Doha, Qatar.

LIGHTING THE WAY
The **largest floor lamp** is 30 feet high and was created by Fredrik Raddum and Martin Raddum in Oslo, Norway!

Located at a temple in Kato City, Japan, the **largest standing lantern** is made of stone and stands 39 feet, 4 inches tall and 24 feet, 3 inches wide.

The **tallest lantern** was 69 feet, 4.67 inches! It was made for the first Wuhan-Chengdu International Giant Panda Lantern Show in Wuhan City, China, in 2012. It depicted the famous Yellow Crane Tower located in Wuhan, Hubei, China.

The **largest display of lanterns** in a single place was 47,759 in Taiwan's Tainan Science Park in 2008. The traditional paper lanterns covered an area of around 269 square feet!

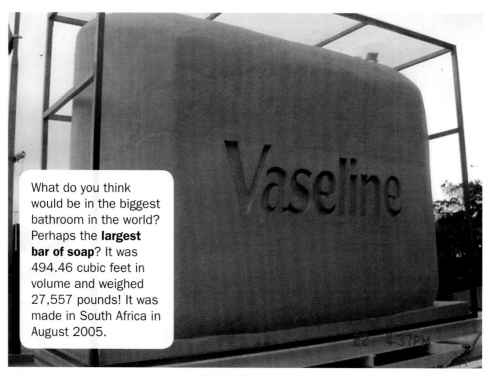

What do you think would be in the biggest bathroom in the world? Perhaps the **largest bar of soap**? It was 494.46 cubic feet in volume and weighed 27,557 pounds! It was made in South Africa in August 2005.

The **largest tube of toothpaste** was 9 feet, 8.4 inches long and weighed 1,719 pounds. It was displayed in China on September 20, 2005.

Val Kolpakov from Alpharetta, Georgia, owns the **largest collection of toothpaste tubes**. As of 2012, he had 2,037 different tubes of toothpaste!

The **longest line of toothpaste tubes** is 2,138 and was created by students of John Carroll University in Ohio on April 13, 2015.

The **largest toilet paper roll** was 9 feet, 8.9 inches in diameter and stood 8 feet, 5.9 inches high.

The **tallest toilet-paper-roll pyramid** stood at 13 feet, 5 inches. It was constructed by Brazilians Ivan Zarif Neto, Rafael Migani Monteiro, and Fernando Gama!

The world's **smallest toilet**, made by scientist Takahashi Kaito of Japan, is less than a nanometer wide!

The **largest whoopee cushion** measures 19 feet, 9.48 inches in diameter and was created by What Now of New Zealand on September 28, 2014. It took up to 15 people pushing down on the classic prankster's toy to deflate it!

It's time you heard about the world's **largest clock**. Using green lasers for the arms, Jim Bowers created a clock face that spanned 3.25 square miles. The timepiece was a showstopping installation at 2011's Burning Man Festival, an event held annually in the Black Rock Desert in Nevada.

The **smallest newspaper** ever was an edition of *Terra Nostra* from Portugal. It was only about seven-tenths of a square inch in area and weighed about the same as a paperclip. It was an exact copy of the normal publication, and they sold 3,000 copies of the tiny edition.

The **heaviest single issue of a newspaper** was the September 13, 1987, edition of the Sunday *New York Times*. It weighed more than 12 pounds and had 1,612 pages.

The **largest magazine**, a copy of *Veronica Magazine* from the Netherlands, stood 8 feet, 10 inches tall and 6 feet, 2 inches wide. It was published to celebrate the magazine's 35th anniversary.

The **smallest magazine cover** is a nano-size etching of *National Geographic Kids* that measures 11 by 14 micrometers. It was etched by a chisel whose tip was 100,000 times smaller than a sharpened pencil point!

If you need to find your place in the big world, this atlas might be a good place to start. The **largest atlas** is *Earth Platinum*, published by Millennium House of Australia. It is more than 6 feet high and 4 feet, 9 inches wide. It weighs around 441 pounds and contains 61 pages of maps. There are only 31 copies, and if you want to buy one, you'll need to shell out $100,000!

The **largest comic strip** was more than 40,745 square feet in area! It was a comic strip about the Japanese soccer team, created to cheer them on as they entered the 2010 World Cup.

The **largest comic book published** is chapter one of the graphic novel *CruZader: Agent of the Vatican*, by Omar Morales. It was measured in Fremont, California, on August 30, 2014. The full-color 28-page work was printed in a run of 105 copies and made available at a cover price of $200 in the US, with a size of 2 feet by 3 feet, 1.19 inches.

The **largest coloring book** measured 107.63 square feet on May 24, 2014. It was created by the Green Owl children's book publisher of Poland, also known as Wydawnictwo Zielona Sowa.

The **largest pop-up book** really popped—the images that sprung out of it stood 7 feet, 9 inches tall! Made by Belgian optician company, Pearle Opticiens, the book itself was titled *My Word* and had pages that were 13 feet, 1 inch by 9 feet, 10 inches.

The **largest book published** was an edition of *The Little Prince* that stood 6 feet, 7 inches high and 10 feet, 1 inch wide when open. It had 128 pages. It was published by Ediouro Publicações of Brazil.

Made by Zollner Elektronic of Germany, the **largest walking robot** is a terrifying dragon that stretches 51 feet, 6 inches from snout to tail and stands 26 feet, 10 inches off the ground. It's so realistic that it even breathes fire!

The **largest robot** moves concrete for a living—a big job for a big robot! It's 231 feet tall with a 250-foot boom. It has two buckets that can move over 6,000 cubic feet of concrete every hour.

But it's the **smallest humanoid robot** that will really win your heart. The BeRobot, made in Taiwan, is only 6 inches high, but it can walk, kick, and even do push-ups!

SECTIO SEVEN

AWESOME ACHIEVEMENTS

All of the largest and smallest records in this book have one thing in common—they were all achieved by totally amazing people. Sometimes the people themselves are the record, too. Whether it's something they can grow, like a beard, something big they can do, like spin a giant Hula-Hoop, or even the size of their own bodies—these awesome people are all larger than life.

The **largest Hula-Hoop workout** had 407 people all Hula-Hooping at once. It was achieved by North Lanarkshire Leisure with Powerhoop Innertrak of the UK, in 2013.

Ever tried to make a lasso with a rope? It's not easy. Kimberly Mink set the record for **largest trick roping loop by a female**, when she spun a loop around herself that measured 76 feet, 2 inches from the eye of the rope to her hand.

Charlie Keyes holds the record for the **largest trick roping loop by a male**. His loop was even greater at 107 feet, 2 inches.

The **tallest Mohawk spike** belongs to Kazuhiro Watanabe of Japan. It stands 4 feet above his head!

The **longest hair** on a woman belongs to Xie Qiuping of China. Her locks reach 18 feet, 5.54 inches long. She stopped cutting her hair when she was 13 years old.

Alan Edward Labbe from Massachusetts has the **largest male Afro** at 5.75 inches high, 8.5 inches wide, and over 5 feet around.

Aevin Dugas from New Orleans has the **largest female Afro** at 6.3 inches high, 8.27 inches wide, and 4 feet, 7 inches around.

The **longest mustache** belongs to Ram Singh Chauhan of India. His mustache measures an amazing 14 feet long.

The **largest gathering of people with mustaches** took place in St. Paul, Minnesota, in 2010. There were 1,131 people there with 1,131 mustaches!

If you're feeling left out because you don't have a mustache, there's always the **largest gathering of people wearing false mustaches**. In 2013, 2,268 people turned out to set this record, achieved by citizens of Fairfield, Iowa!

The **longest beard on a living person** belongs to Sarwan Singh of Canada. It was last measured at 8 feet, 2.5 inches long!

The **longest beard ever** belonged to Norwegian Hans N. Langseth—when he was buried in 1927, his beard was 17 feet, 6 inches long. The beard is now kept at the Smithsonian Institution.

Vivian Wheeler of the US holds the record for **longest beard on a woman**. It was measured at more than 10 inches long in April 2011.

FACT!
The **longest beard ever on a woman** belonged to the famous bearded lady Janice Deveree. It measured 14 inches in 1884.

Long hair, long mustache, long beard . . . how about a long tongue? The **longest tongue on a woman** belongs to Chanel Tapper of California. Her tongue is 3.8 inches from the middle of her top lip to the tip.

The **longest tongue on a man** is just a lick longer. Nick Stoeberl's tongue is 3.97 inches from lip to tip. He can even paint with it!

Byron Schlenker has the **widest tongue** on record. It's 3.37 inches at its broadest point.

LAPPING UP THE RECORDS!

Thomas Blackthorne from the UK can lift 27 pounds, 8.96 ounces with his tongue—that's the **heaviest weight ever lifted by a tongue**. The weight was attached by a hook—ouch!

The **largest gape**—the distance from the tips of his top teeth to the tips of his bottom teeth with the mouth totally open—is JJ Bittner's at 3.4 inches.

Big tongues call for big mouths! Without stretching, the **widest mouth** measures 6.69 inches and belongs to Francisco Domingo Joaquim "Chiquinho" from Angola. It was measured on the set of *Lo Show dei Record* in Rome, Italy, in 2010.

FACT!
There are accounts of a man named Thomas Wedders who had a nose 7.5 inches long, so he holds the record for **longest nose ever**.

Mehmet Ozyurek of Turkey has the **longest nose on a living person**—it's 3.46 inches from bridge to tip.

The **longest fingernails on a woman ever** belonged to Lee Redmond, whose nails were 28 feet, 4.5 inches in 2008. It took her 48 hours to paint her massive nails.

The **longest fingernails ever** belonged to Melvin Boothe, whose nails had a combined length of 32 feet, 3.8 inches.

Chris "The Dutchess" Walton has the current record for the **longest fingernails on a woman**. They total 23 feet, 11 inches in length as of 2013.

The **largest foot rotation** was achieved by Moses Lanham, who can turn his feet 120 degrees away from each other.

He also holds the record for the **fastest time to walk 20 meters** (65 feet, 7.2 inches) **with feet facing backward**: 19.59 seconds.

Because of her enthusiasm for Victorian dress, Cathie Jung used tight-lacing to get the **smallest waist ever**, 15 inches around while wearing a corset.

166

Being big or small doesn't stop these record holders from doing their jobs. The **shortest stand-up comedian** is Imaan Hadchiti of Lebanon and Australia. The 3-foot-4.3-inch man has been performing on the comedy circuit in Australia and the UK for over a decade.

The **shortest professional stuntman** currently working, Kiran Shah of the UK, is 4 feet, 1.7 inches tall and has appeared in 52 movies. He has done stunts for Christopher Reeve in the *Superman* movies and for Elijah Wood in the *Lord of the Rings* trilogy!

Daniele Seccarecci of Italy was the **heaviest ever competitive bodybuilder** in the world. His competition weight was 297 pounds, 9.92 ounces. Sadly, he passed away in 2013.

The **lightest competitive bodybuilder** is Thomas Campion of the UK. He tips the scale at 122 pounds, 5.76 ounces.

The **heaviest sportswoman** is Sharran Alexander of the UK. She weighs 448 pounds and competes all over the world as an amateur sumo wrestler.

The **heaviest living athlete** is also a sumo wrestler. Emmanuel "Manny" Yarborough is 6 feet, 8 inches tall and weighs 704 pounds.

Sun Mingming of China is the **tallest basketball player**. He stands 7 feet, 8.98 inches tall.

Together Sun Mingming and his wife, Xu Yan, make up the **tallest living married couple**! Xu Yan is 6 feet, 1.74 inches tall, making their combined height 13 feet, 10.72 inches.

STANDING TALL!
The **tallest teenager** is Kevin Bradford, 18, from Florida, who measured 7 feet, 1 inch tall on April 30, 2015.

The **tallest teenage girl** is Rumeysa Gelgi of Turkey. On March 19, 2014, she measured 7 feet, 0.009 inches tall.

The **tallest female twins** are identical twins Ann and Claire Recht—they each stand 6 feet, 7 inches tall.

FACT! The **tallest male twins** are also identical, Michael and James Lanier, both 7 feet, 3 inches tall. Both brothers played basketball in college.

The **heaviest twins ever** were Billy Leon and Benny Loyd McCrary, professional tag wrestlers from North Carolina. Billy Leon weighed 743 pounds and Benny Loyd weighed 723 pounds.

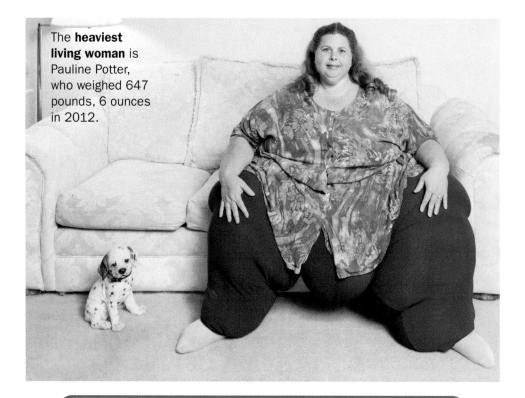

The **heaviest living woman** is Pauline Potter, who weighed 647 pounds, 6 ounces in 2012.

Until recently, the **heaviest man** was Manuel Uribe from Mexico, weighing in at 1,235 pounds. Sadly, he passed away in May 2014. The **heaviest man ever**, though, was Jon Brower Minnoch. He was 6 feet, 1 inch tall and weighed more than 1,400 pounds in 1978.

The **longest legs on a woman** belong to Svetlana Pankratova from Russia, whose legs stretch to 51.9 inches.

FOCUS ON: SULTAN KÖSEN!

At 8 feet, 3 inches, Sultan Kösen of Turkey—the **tallest living man**—is head and shoulders above them all! Sultan didn't start his incredible growth spurt until he was 10 years old, but he appears to have finally stopped growing! Although clothes shopping can be a challenge, Sultan enjoys the benefits of being so tall. He's able to see a great distance and helps to change light bulbs or hang curtains.

THAT'S SOME HANDSHAKE!

Sultan also holds the record for the **largest hands on a living person**. In February 2011, his hands measured 11.22 inches from the wrist to the top of the middle finger. He also has the **widest hand span**—12 inches.

The **tallest man ever**, Robert Pershing Wadlow, was even taller than Sultan at 8 feet, 11.1 inches tall. He also holds the record for the **largest hands ever**. Robert's hands measured 12.75 inches from wrist to fingertip.

The **shortest living woman** is Jyoti Amge from India, who has also previously held the record for **shortest teenage girl**. Jyoti is only 24.7 inches tall—a little over two feet. An actress by profession, she says her dream is to go to Hollywood.

FACT!
The **shortest woman ever**, Pauline Musters, was only a tiny bit smaller—when she died, she was found to be exactly 24 inches.

Unbelievably, Chandra Bahadur Dangi from Nepal was even smaller, standing just 21.5 inches tall. Although he sadly passed away in 2015, he still holds the record for **shortest man ever**.

These lungs don't belong to a real person, but they are the **largest model of a human organ** ever made. They stand 16 feet, 5 inches tall and 18 feet, 11 inches wide. They were created by Pfizer Japan in 2010. Bet making them took a lot of deep breaths.

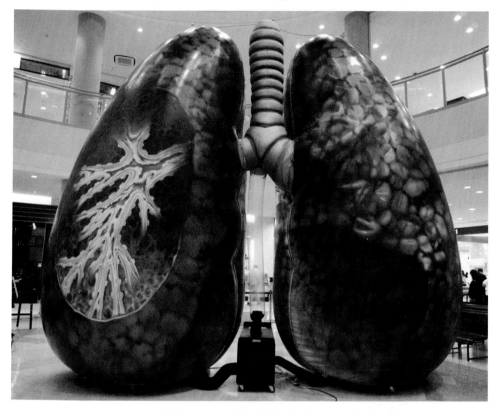

In real life, the **largest organ** of the human body is, of course, the skin. Part of the skin—the fingerprint—was re-created with 250 people at an event organized by Villavicencio Argentina to form the **largest human fingerprint**!

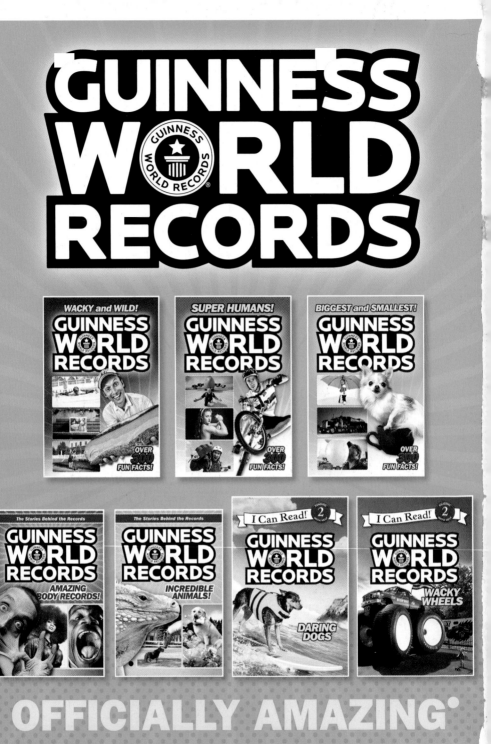

GUINNESS WORLD RECORDS

WACKY and WILD!
GUINNESS WORLD RECORDS
OVER 300 FUN FACTS!

SUPER HUMANS!
GUINNESS WORLD RECORDS
OVER 300 FUN FACTS!

BIGGEST and SMALLEST!
GUINNESS WORLD RECORDS
OVER 300 FUN FACTS!

The Stories Behind the Records
GUINNESS WORLD RECORDS
AMAZING BODY RECORDS!

The Stories Behind the Records
GUINNESS WORLD RECORDS
INCREDIBLE ANIMALS!

I Can Read! 2
GUINNESS WORLD RECORDS
DARING DOGS

I Can Read! 2
GUINNESS WORLD RECORDS
WACKY WHEELS

OFFICIALLY AMAZING°

HARPER
An Imprint of HarperCollinsPublishers

www.hc.com/guinnessworldrecords